I invite you to the magical land of sounds which is called MUSIC. It is hard to imagine a modern world without music, because it surrounds us everywhere. For the beginner musicians, this land is full of mysteries and puzzles. How do we solve them? This is where the LANGUAGE OF SOUNDS comes into the picture! Let this book help you open the door to another world, where one can not go without words. Welcome!

Today we will study about the large city inside the grand piano. Open the piano lid and our instrument can tell us about everything, any mood, image or character may be created with it.

It was late autumn, and a girl came to the shop together with her parents. She really liked this beautiful snow-white grand piano. Her mother said, "But you cannot play the piano!" But the girl was unstoppable because she liked that instrument so much. A little while later, the grand piano was at their apartment. The girl ran to it and hit the keys forcefully, which hurt the instrument so much. Music got scared and it hid itself.

All of a sudden, there was a knock at the door, and the little girl's grandmother came. She was a violin fairy, but she also could play the piano. When her magical fingers touched the keys, a marvelous tune played, and it showed the whole beauty... The piano was unbelievably happy. This way, music worked wonders, and the girl seriously decided to learn it.

Try pressing the piano key

They are three registers:

bears   fox   birds

but the piano is magical, so everyone has their own heroes, and what are yours?

the lower
register ....

the middle
register ....

the higher
register ....

There are white and black keys, and all together they are called a keyboard. Black keys make groups of 2 and 3.

Show all the groups of two black keys and then of three.

Now let's play a game

Close your eyes, touch the keyboard, and guess which group of black keys is under your hand. Is it the group two or three black keys?

I'm sure you figured that one!

To get to the next page you need to go through the maze

Hand position and pose

There are three support points: your feet, the chair and your fingers

Sit up straight, curl your fingers (as if you were holding a small ball) and put support on your feet.

Every finger has its own name and number.
Let's label your fingers with different colours.

And now try to play the C note on the keyboard with your third finger.

Walk around the keyboard with your second finger

Imagine that we are in the forest, we are walking and first we see a bear (he is kind, we are not afraid of him), then we meet a fox and she also wants to go with us, but she can't, because she is in a different register. And finally we walked out of the forest and hear the singing of birds, who sing their melody

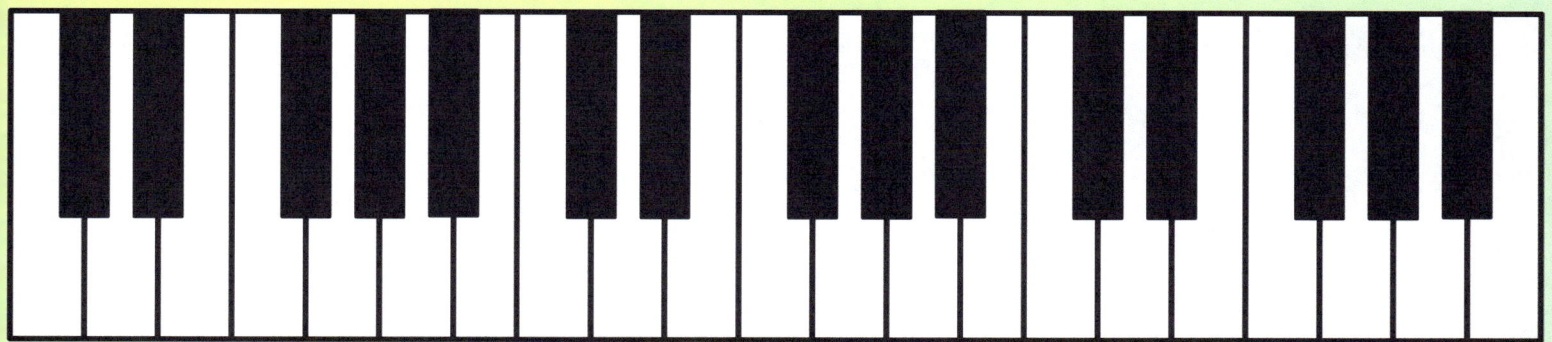

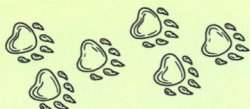

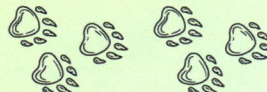

Walk on the keyboard with 2 and 3 fingers (from bears to birds)

Help the bear find the honey. Colour all the squares in order from one to ten and make way to the honey.

	1	3	5	8
	2	3	8	9
2	4	9	4	7	3
3	2	6	5	8	2
5	4	7	10		
9	10	8	9		

Musical notation

Task: Draw the Treble Clef Queen

Once upon a time there lived a king and a queen. The queen's name was **Treble Clef**. She was very remarkable and always stood at the beginning of the stave. **Treble Clef** was very elegant and often looked like a violin.

The queen has a king, whose name was **Bass Clef**. He was used to mark the notes of the lower register (lower sounds). He was very serious and fat, and people compared him to a contrabass. As any keys, they opened the door to a wonderful land called music.

Make markings on the keyboard. Separate each octave

Play two notes next to each other with your second and third fingers

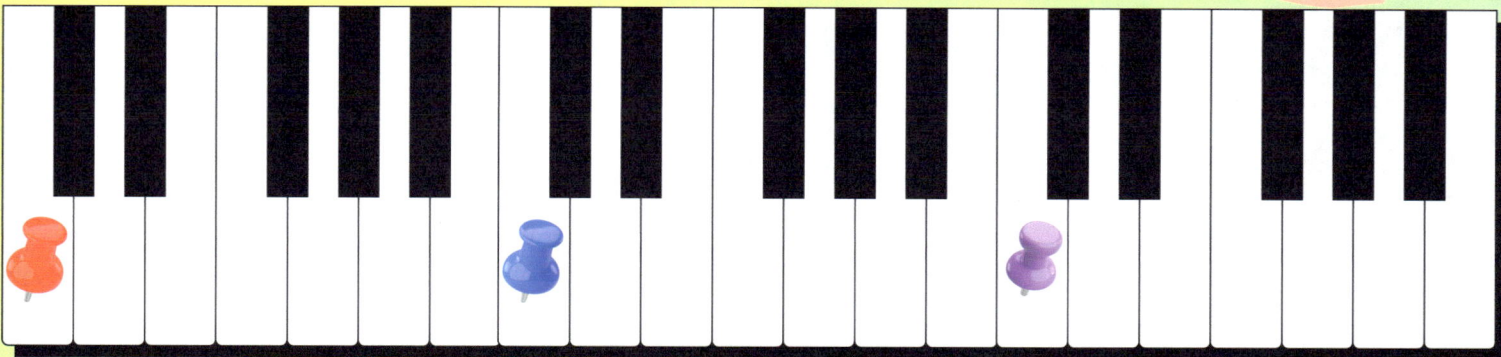

EXAMPLE

C–D–C–D

D–E–D–E

E–F–E–F

NOW SING THESE NOTES AND PLAY

repeat every day !

Play notes next to each other with your first and second fingers

Now change to the third and fourth fingers, play two notes located next to each other

Try singing like that too

EXAMPLE

C–D–C–D

D–E–D–E

E–F–E–F

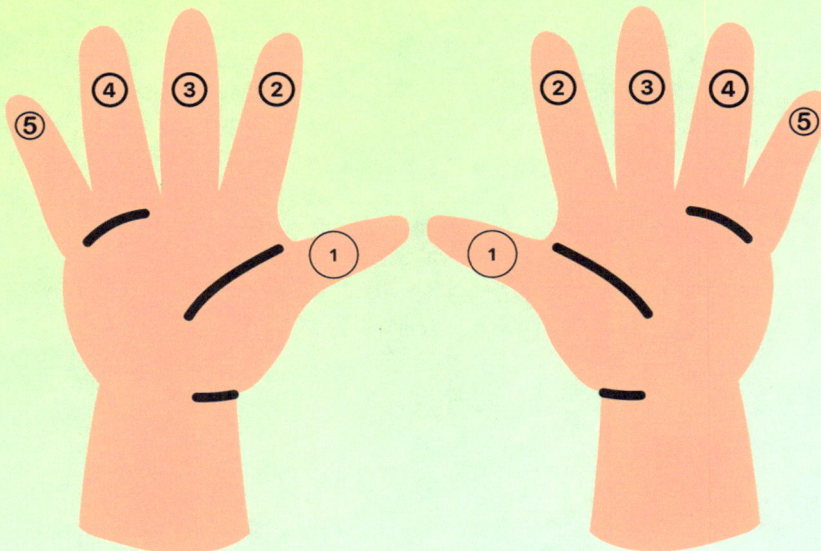

repeat every day **!**

Now we will go from the first finger to the fifth

① ② ③ ④ ⑤

EXAMPLE

We climb up the hill

C-D-E-F-G

Please note: your fingers should be close to the black keys.

We go down the hill

G-F-E-D-C

repeat every day !

Now we are trying to play staccato

Imagine that the piano is dirty and you want to shake the dust off it.

First we start with the second finger, play the same note several times

EXAMPLE

C-C-C-C-C

D-D-D-D-D

Now the third, fourth and fifth

Tap each finger gently on the key

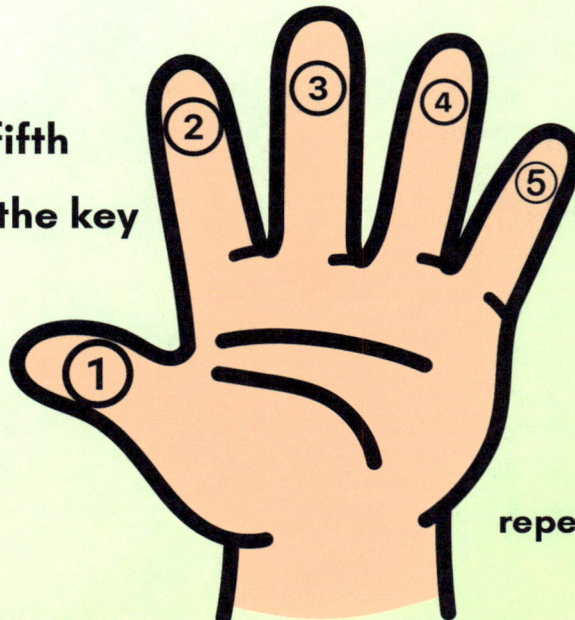

repeat every day !

They had a very big family and had seven little children. They lived in a large castle, where every child had a floor.

.... **B** ♪

.... *A* ♪

.... G ♪

F ♪ ....

E ♪ ....

D ♪ ....

C ♪ ....

C lived on an added line. **D** lived on the next floor and **E** on the first line. **F** always looked out of the window and **G** sat on the line. **A** and **B** sat on the highest floors. Let's think of names for them...

20

C D E F G A B

Notes arrived to their new home but C was late and was left alone. No place remained on lines and C received some good advice "Stay right there, on the added line and it will be just as good."

D is really scared of heights and was really nervous. That is why it always lives under the first line.

E is just a little higher. You should know it; I'm no liar. Living on the first of lines Should it be very fine?

F is in a fancy place. Between the first and second line, going lower is so boring and going higher is no fun.

G is one on the second line, and this place is the best it got. It waters flowers from the top using a pretty flower pot.

Now, the frolic note of A is between lines two and three. It sings all the songs it knows, making its friends joyful, you see!

"And where's the note called B?" Someone asked me politely. Look up there, it's higher, see? On the line that's numbered three!

Musical rhythm

Now we will enter the realm of the maestro of rhythm.

Musical rhythm is like the heartbeat of music.

Think of rhythm as being like the steps when you walk. If you walk fast, the steps are frequent and quick.

if slowly - the steps are rare and smooth.

Let's try clapping your hands at a
steady pace, like clock's ticking.
One, two, three...

Game

Now let's sing a song syllable by
syllable.

Ti-ger, ti-ger,
Burn-ing bright,
In the for-est
Of the night.

Red and yel-low,
Pink and green,
Pur-ple, or-ange,
Blue I've seen.

Lit-tle lamb,
Soft and white,
Play-ing in
The morn-ing light.

Win-ter chill,
Snow-flakes fall,
Frost-y winds
En-vel-op all.

Help the children find the apple

This kingdom was guarded by large cats, which could transform into enormous black columns. The first column was called 'Two Black Keys' and it guarded the notes C, D, and E. The second, even larger than the first was called 'Three Black Keys' and guarded the remaining four notes.

Sometimes, weather was bad in the magical kingdom, and all its residents were sad. In the language of music it's called **minor**.

But mainly, joy and cheer were in this kingdom, and the sun shone almost every day. Everybody was happy and called this **major**.

Play with the second, third and fourth finger on the three black keys play with each finger separately

After you have played each note separately, play three notes in a row.

Example

2-3-4-3-2

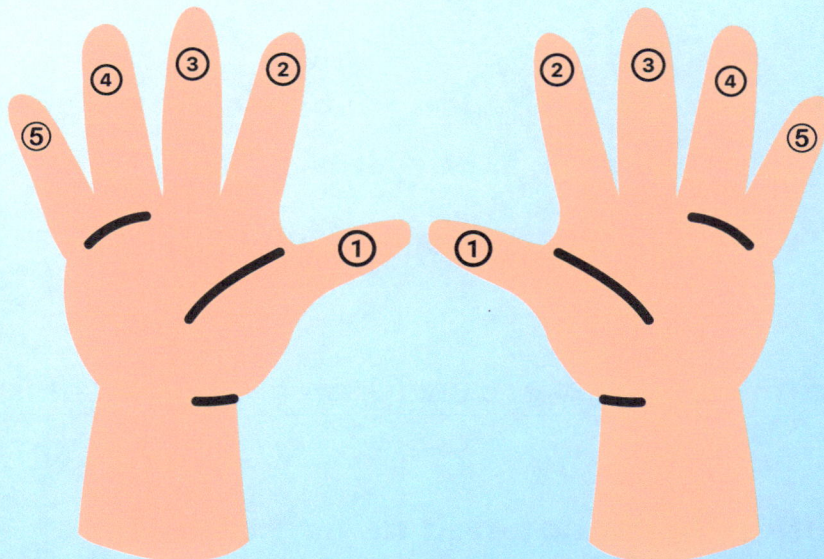

Use the second and third fingers to play on two black keys

repeat every day

27

Duration of notes

As you and I have determined, we have high and low sounds, and they can also be fast and slow.

We shared an orange, there are many of us and only one of it

A whole orange — Whole note

Two halves of an orange — Half notes

Four orange slices — Quarter notes

Eight orange slices — Eighth notes

A whole note **O** is the longest note, counted in 4 counts (one, two, three, four)

Half note ♩ - counted in two

$$\text{half} + \text{half} = \text{O}$$

A quarter note ♩ counts as one beat (time)

$$\text{quarter} + \text{quarter} + \text{quarter} + \text{quarter} = \text{O}$$

The eighth note ♪ is counted as half a count.

$$♪+♪+♪+♪+♪+♪+♪+♪ = \text{O}$$

$$♫ + ♫ + ♫ + ♫ = \text{O}$$

We knock a whole note 4 times – one, two, three, four.

We knock the half note twice – one, two

We knock the quarter note once

We knock the eighth note half times

Clap your hands rhythm

E	D	C	D	E	E	E
Ma – ry	had	a	lit – tle	lamb,		

D	D	D	E	G	G
lit – tle	lamb,	lit – tle	lamb,		

repeat every day

Position of notes of treble clef.

Task: Write down the notes.

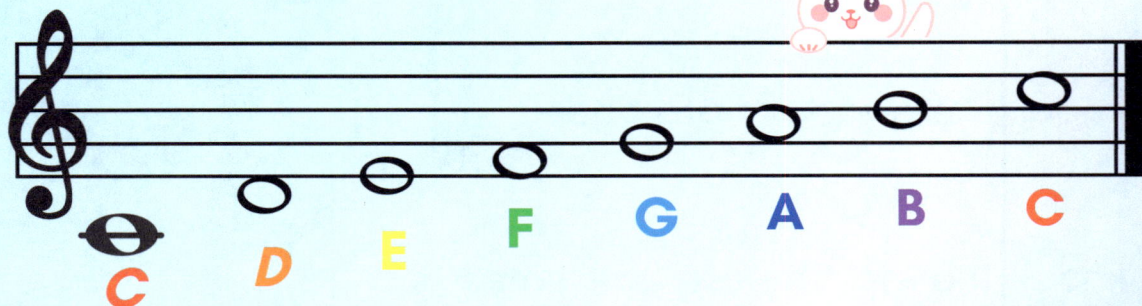

C D E F G A B C

Cross out the incorrectly written notes.

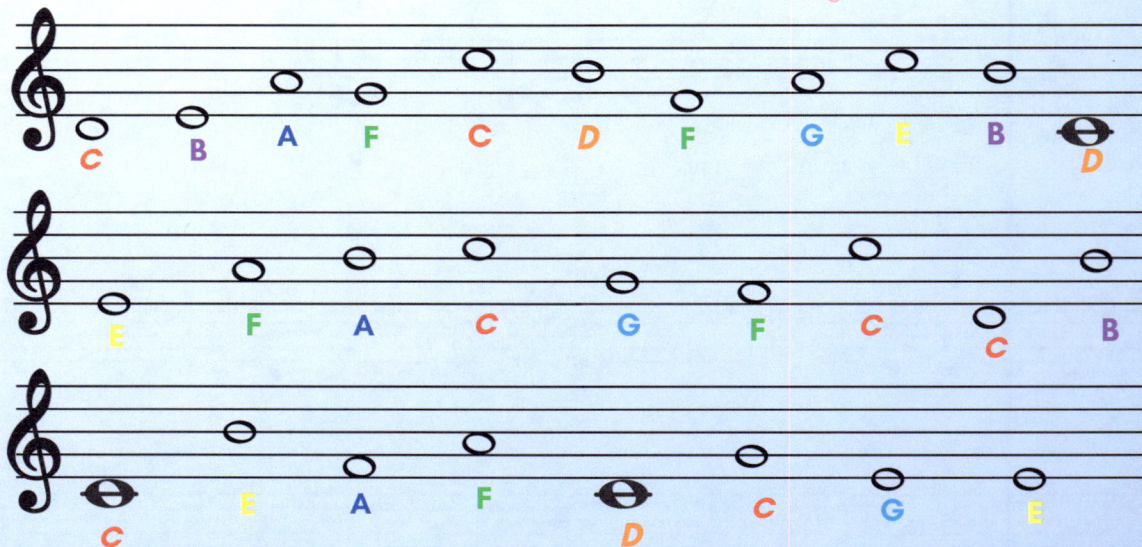

C B A F C D F G E B D

E F A C G F C C B

C E A F D C G E

A   F   D   G   A   E   C   B

D   C   A   B   E   C   E   F   G

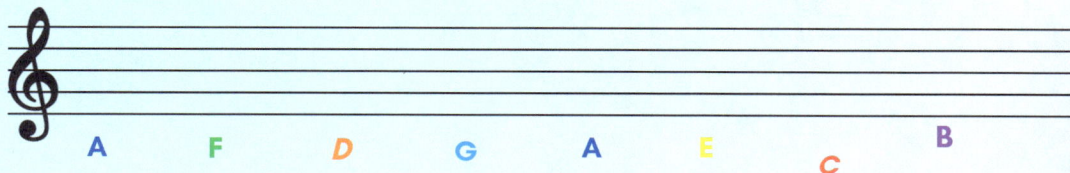

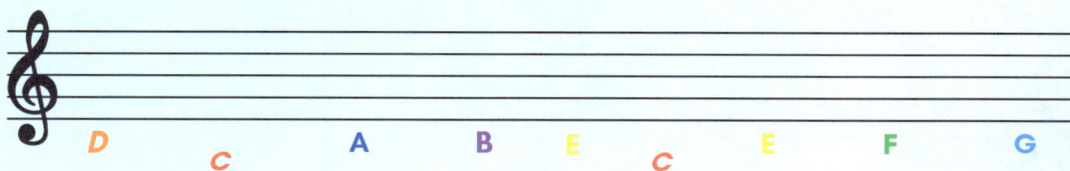

Location of notes on the keyboard.

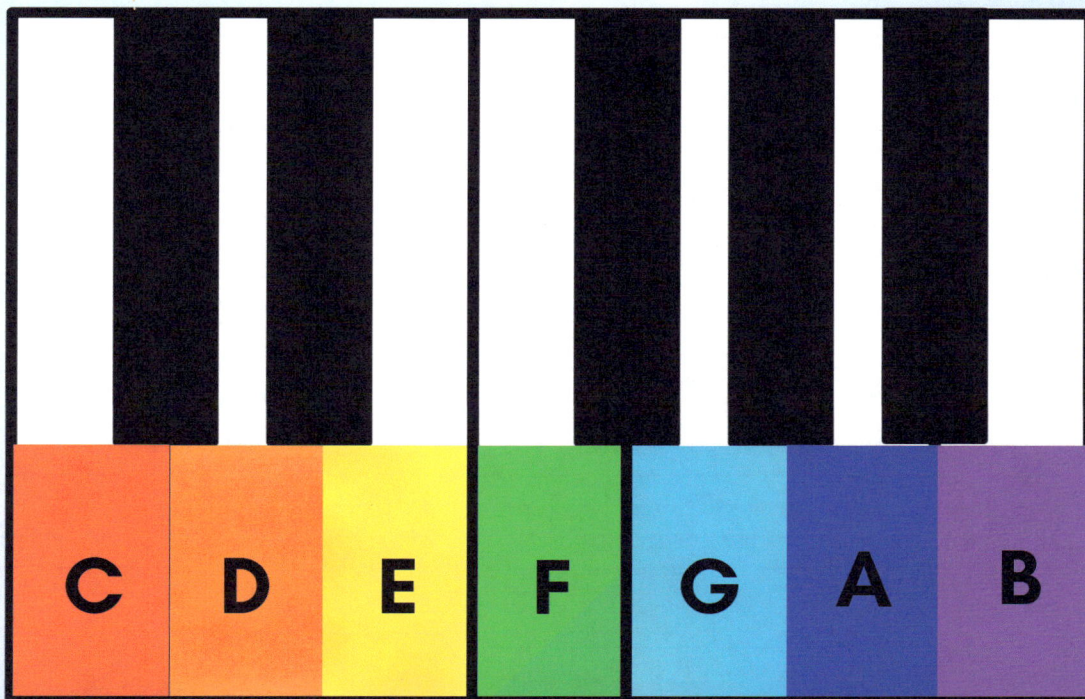

C D E F G A B

F is in Space 1

A is in Space 2

F   F   F   A   A   A

Write the name of each note

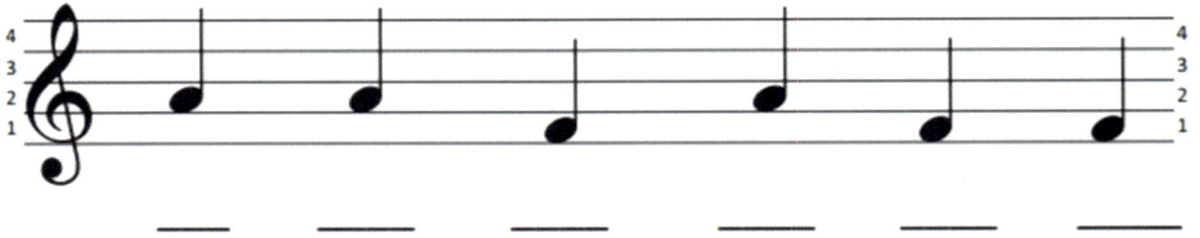

___   ___   ___   ___   ___   ___

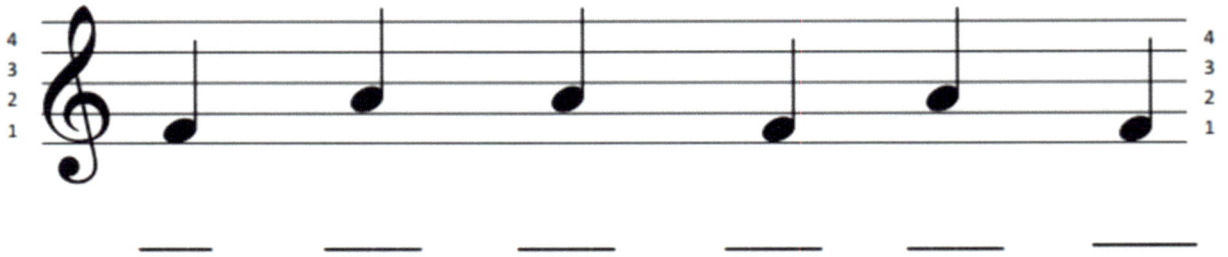

___   ___   ___   ___   ___   ___

Draw 3 F notes

Draw 3 A notes

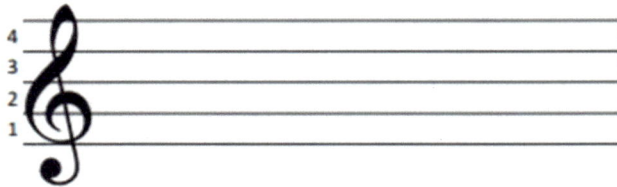
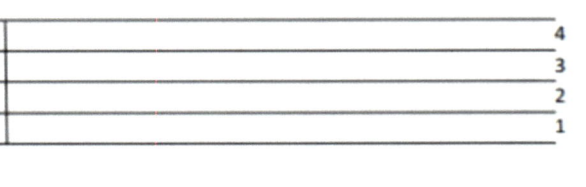

E is on Line 1   G is on Line 2

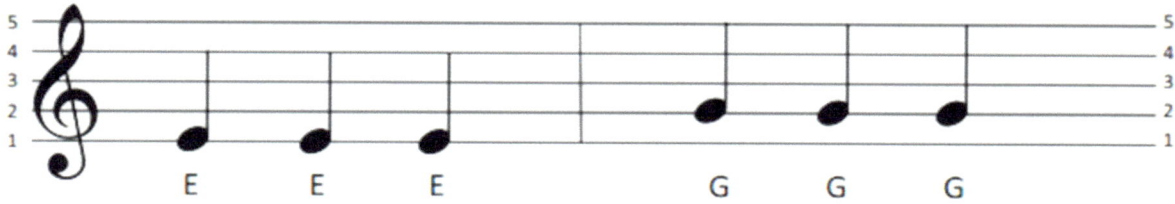

E   E   E   G   G   G

Write the name of each note

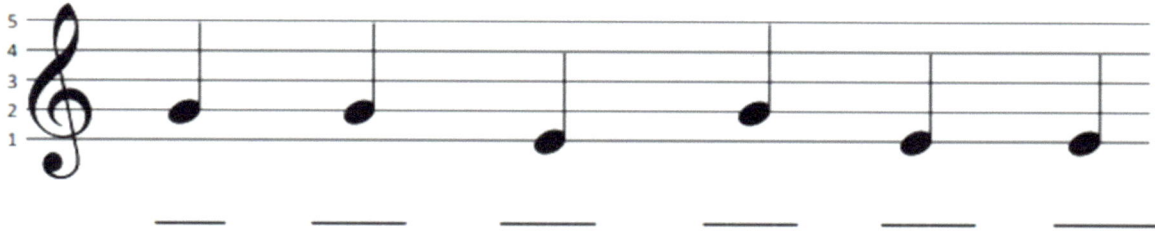

____ ____ ____ ____ ____ ____

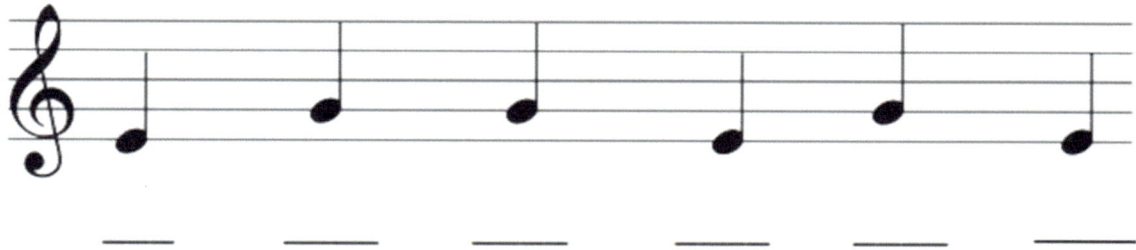

____ ____ ____ ____ ____ ____

Draw 3 E notes   Draw 3 G notes

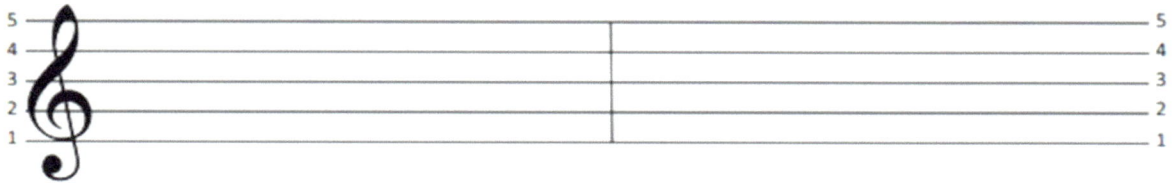

1.

2.

3.

4.

5.

Notes are lost in space
help find their names

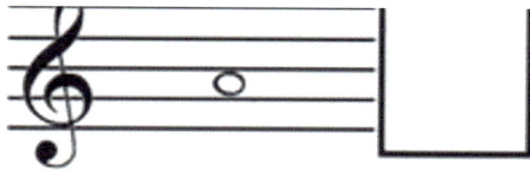

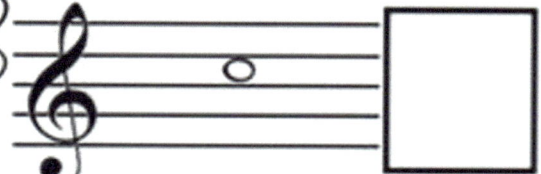

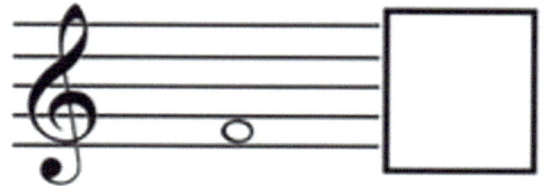

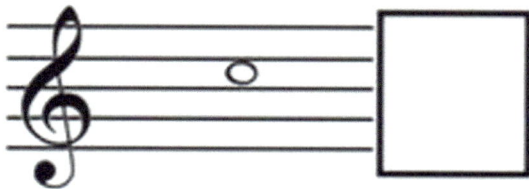

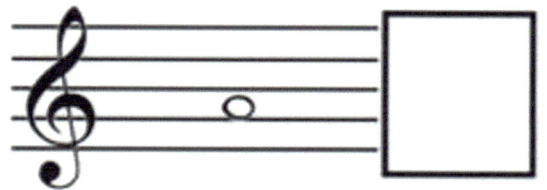

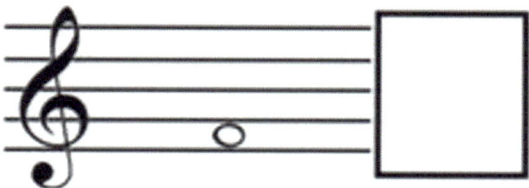

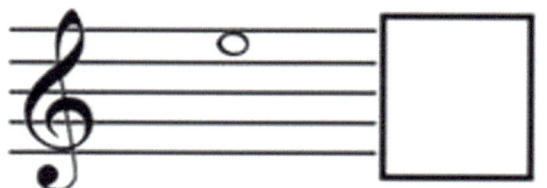

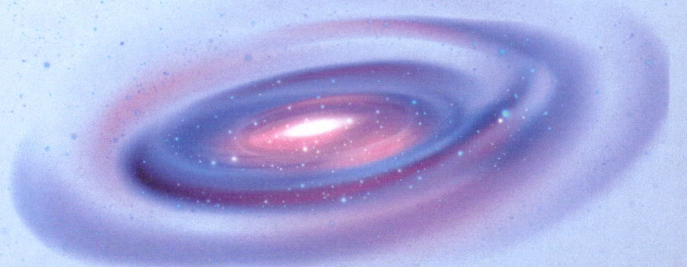

Cross out the notes that are written incorrectly.

The arrangement of notes in the treble clef

C D E F G A B C D E F G A B C

First octave
(contra octave)

Second octave

The arrangement of notes in the bass clef

C D E F G A B C D E F G A B C

Great octave

Small octave

The task is to find the notes on the keyboard: C,D,G,B

Show the notes C, F, A, B, E, D, G on the piano

Write down the notes

Treble clef

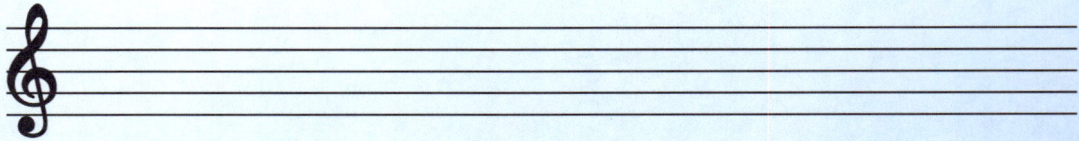

Bass clef

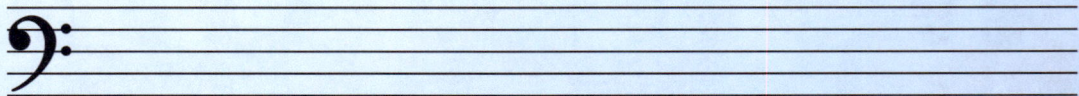

2 6 3 1 7 5 4

Notes in treble clef

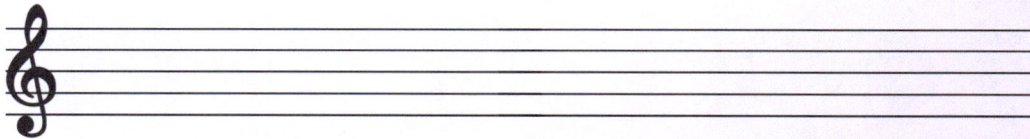

Bass clef notes

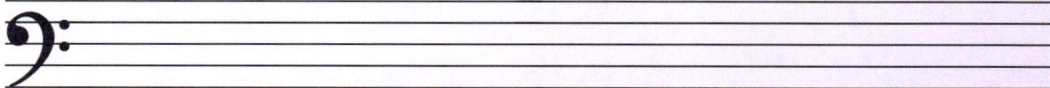

There are only seven notes in the world

C, D, E, F, G, A, B.

Remember these notes and quickly name them.

Colour the autumn leaves.
C: red. D: orange. E: yellow. F: green. G: pink. A: blue.
B: purple.

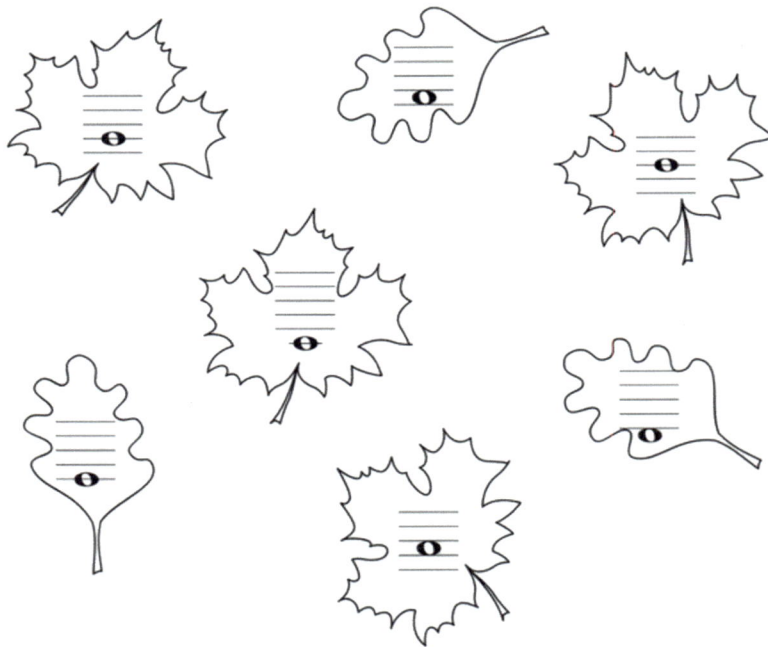

C - red, D - orange, E - yellow, G - blue, A - pink, B - purple.

Color the balls on the Christmas tree.

Task
Spelling of musical symbols

Whole notes

Half notes

Quarter notes

Eighth notes

Task
Spelling of musical symbols

Eighth notes

A whole pause   **Half pause**

Quarter pause   **Eighth pause**

43

Game
Draw the duration that is hidden in the circle

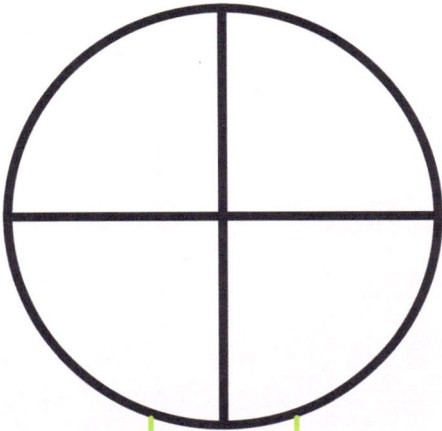

Decode the crossword and go to the next magical page.

1. Keyboard musical instrument...

2. How do you say loud in magic language?

3. How do you say sad in musical language?

4. What is the word fun in musical language?

5. The heartbeat of music is...

6. A symbol used to write musical sounds...

7. Note G is located on which line?

Play the melody on the piano and draw a picture to the melodies

After a long journey through the pages of the musical country, each note finally found its place and began to create its own melody.

How do you imagine this song?
Draw a picture

Mary Had a Little Lamb

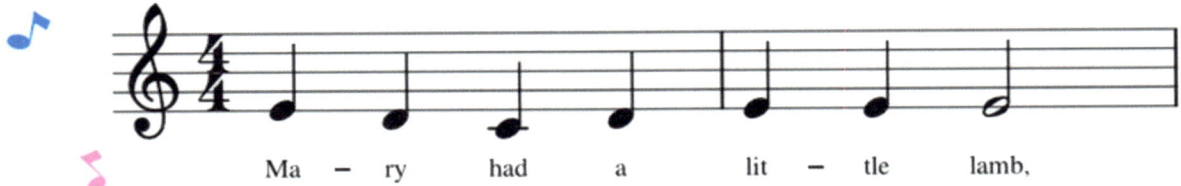

Ma — ry   had   a   lit — tle   lamb,

lit — tle   lamb,   lit — tle   lamb,

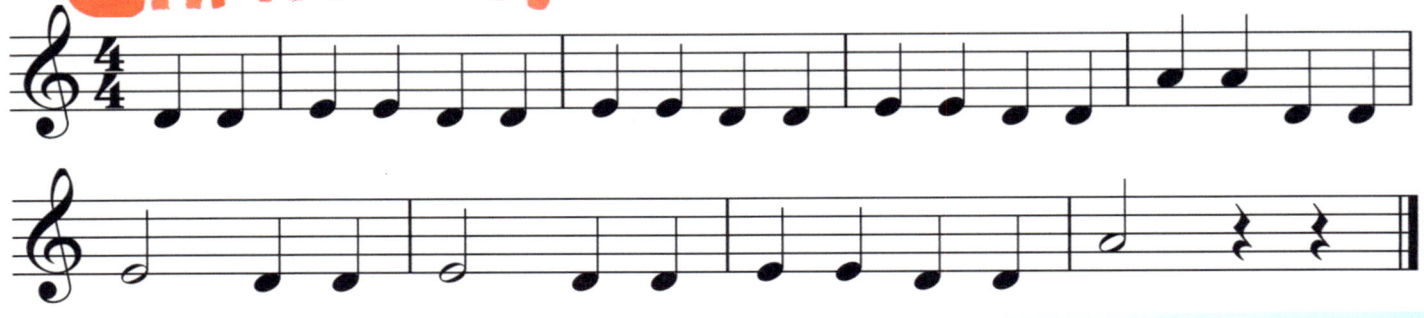

50

Christmas tree

BIRD SONG

As the black-bird in the Spring,

'neath the wil-low tree.

sing of Aur-a Lee.

Aur-a Lee, Aur-a Lee,

Go Tell Aunt Rhody

Go   tell   aunt   Rho - dy,

go   tell   aunt   Rho - dy,

go   tell   aunt   Rho - dy   the

old   grey   goose   is   here

London Bridge

Lon - don bridge is fall - ing down,

fall - ing down, fall - ing down,

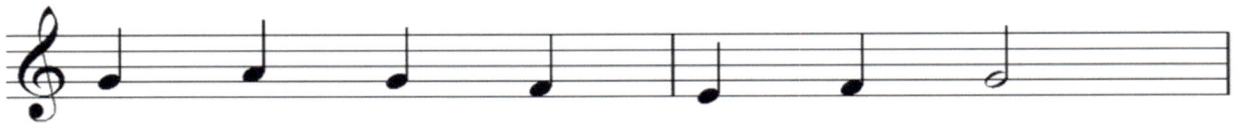

Lon - don bridge is fall - ing down,

my fair la - dy.

New Year

Lullaby

Old MacDonald Had a Farm

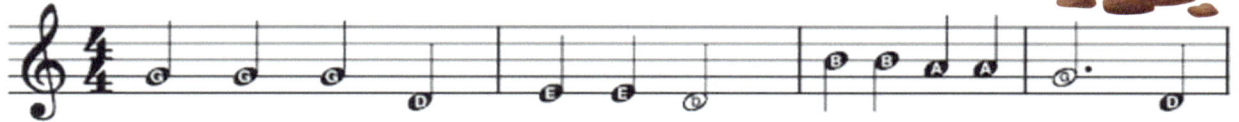

Old Mac-Do-nald had a farm, E I E I O and

on his farm he had some cows, E I E I O. With a

moo moo here and a moo moo there, here a moo, there a moo,

Bingo

There was a far-mer, had a dog, and Bin-go was his

name - o. B I N G O,

B I N G O, B I

N G O, and Bin-go was his name - o!

LOU

E	C	E	E	E	G

Lou,   Lou,   skip   to   my   Lou.

Lou,   Lou,   skip   to   my   Lou.

Lou,   Lou,   skip   to   my   Lou.

Skip   to   my   Lou   my   dar   -   ling.

Ode To Joy

Alphabet

A B C D E F G, H I J K

L M N O P, Q R S, T U V,

W_____ X, Y & Z, now I know my

A B Cs, next time won't you sing with me?

how I won - der what you are.

All Through the Night

All   through   the   night,   the

moon   is   sil - ver   bright.

Crick - et sings his   ti - ny song,

sings   it through the   whole night long,

All   through   the   night.

THE CLOCK SONG

Grand - fa-ther's clock goes Tick tock, tick tock, tick tock.

Mu-mmy's ki-tchen clock goes Tick tock tick tock tick tock tick tock

My lit tle watch goes Tick tick tick tick tick tick tick tick

tick tick tick tick tick tick tick tick STOP!

Twinkle, Twinkle, Little Star

Twin - kle, twin - kle, lit - tle star,

how I won - der what you are.

Up a - bove the world so high,

like a dia - mond in the sky.

Twin - kle, twin - kle, lit - tle star,

Jingle Bells

Jin - gle bells, jin - gle bells,

jin - gle all the way,

Oh what fun it is to ride in a

one - horse o - pen sleigh, hey!

jin - gle all the way,

Jin - gle bells, jin - gle bells,

Oh what fun it is to ride in a

one - horse o - pen sleigh.

The bunny wants to go to the next page so much, help him by coloring it

Remember when we went up the magical staircase and discovered new notes?

B
A
G
F
E
D
C

Every step is a note. If you stand on a step and want to go half a step higher, it is called sharp. Sharp makes the sound of the note half a tone higher.

For instance, when you play the piano and press the white C key and then the black key immediately to the right of it, it is C sharp.

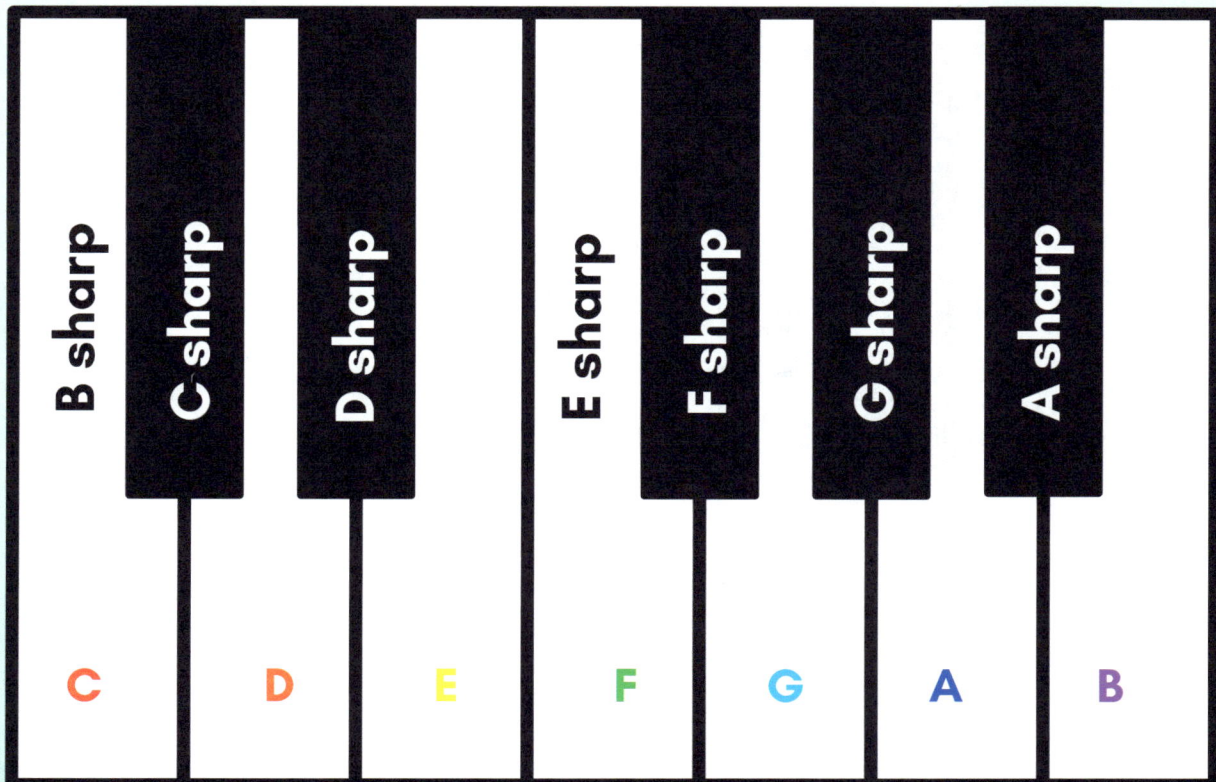

\#

B sharp   C sharp   D sharp   E sharp   F sharp   G sharp   A sharp

C   D   E   F   G   A   B

Now imagine that you want to go half a step lower. This is called flat. Flat makes the sound of the note half a tone lower. For instance, if you play the white D key and then the black key immediately to the left of it, it is D flat.

There is also such a magical sign - NATYRAL. It cancels the effect of the flat or sharp sign

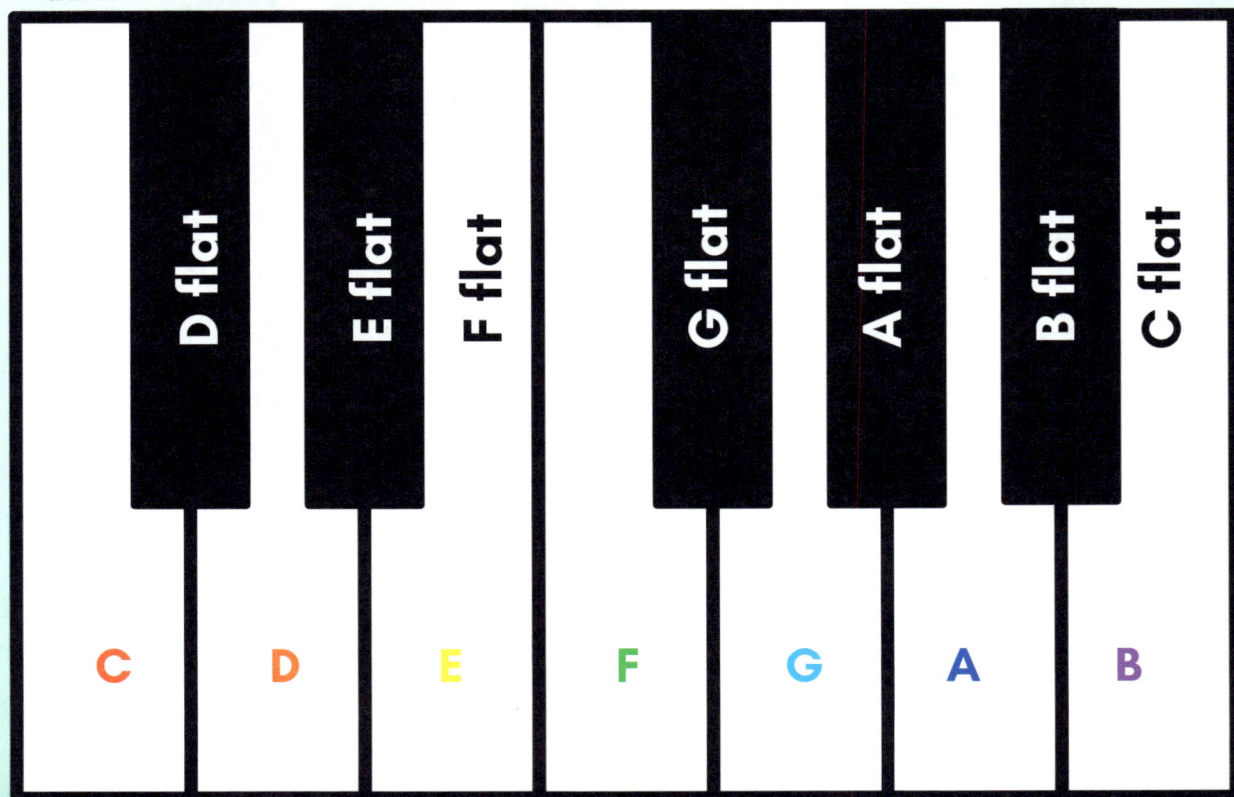

SHARP   FLATS

D flat   E flat   F flat   G flat   A flat   B flat   C flat

C   C   D   E   F   G   A   B

Happy birthday

Fur Elise

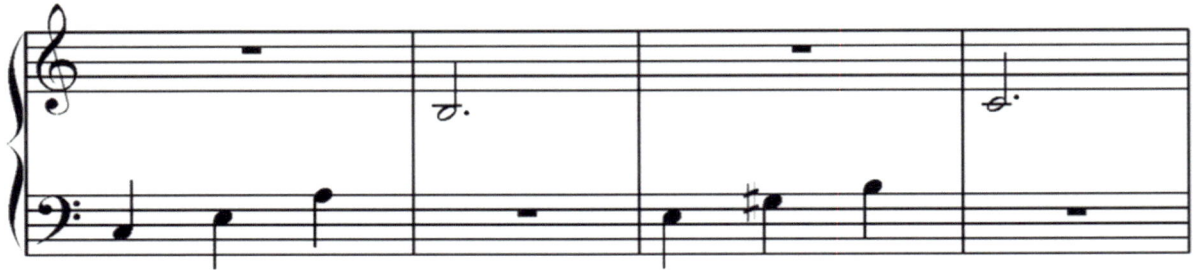

The bear wants to go to the next page so much, help him by coloring it

At the beginning of the piece, right after the treble or bass clef, sharps or flats may be placed. These signs are called key signs and indicate the key of the piece.

Order of sharps and flats of treble clef and bass clef

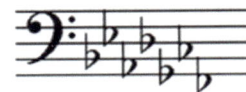

These signs mean which notes are going to be half a tone higher during the whole piece, if there are no other indications.

Write the music signs down.

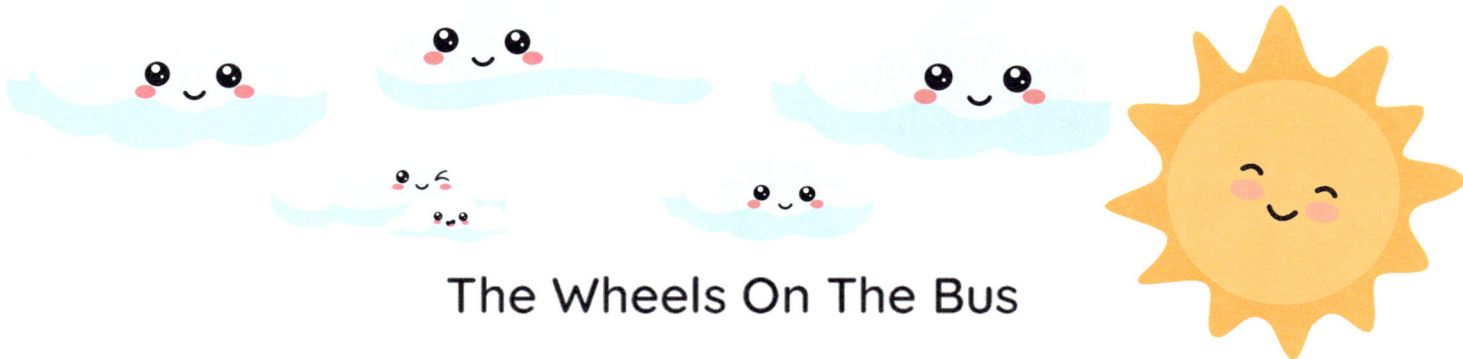

The Wheels On The Bus

The wheels on the bus go round and round,

round and round, round and round, the

wheels on the bus go round and round,

all through the town.

What is gamma?

A scale is like a staircase of notes. We start with one note, move up the steps (or down the steps), and return to where we started. For example, if we play a C major scale, we start with the note "C", move up through all the notes (D, E, F, G, A, B), and return to "C" again.

C D E F G A B C

Go from note C to C of the next octave

C   C

Gammas come with both sharps (#) and flats (♭). It depends on the gamma key.

Gamma with sharps have raised notes (a sharp is added)

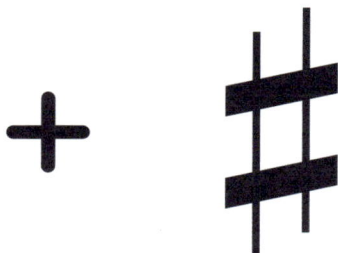

$+$ #

Gamma with flats have lower notes (a flat is added)

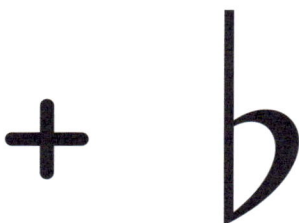

$+$ ♭

Example

Gamma G major(F♯)

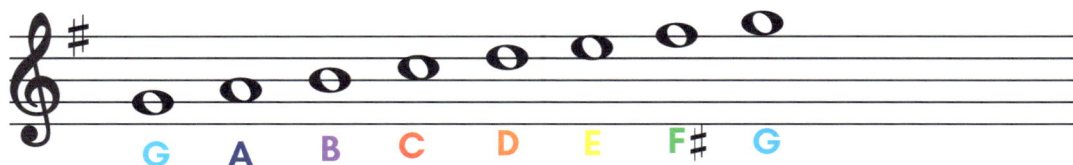

G A B C D E F♯ G

Gamma F major(B♭)

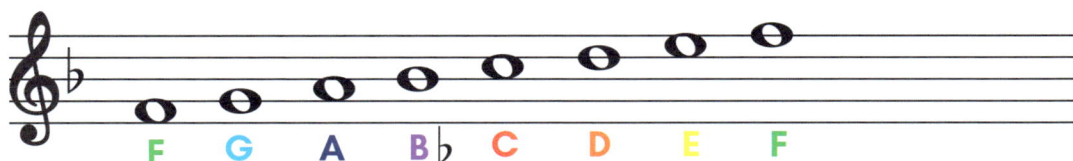

F G A B♭ C D E F

Complete the tune and write illustration to the tunes.

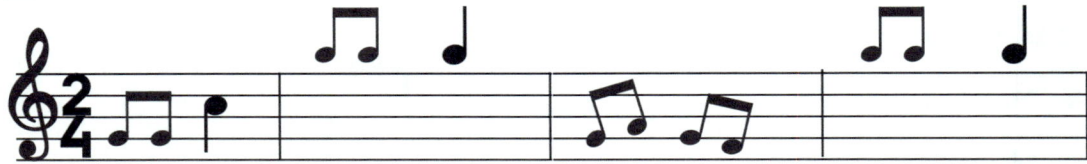

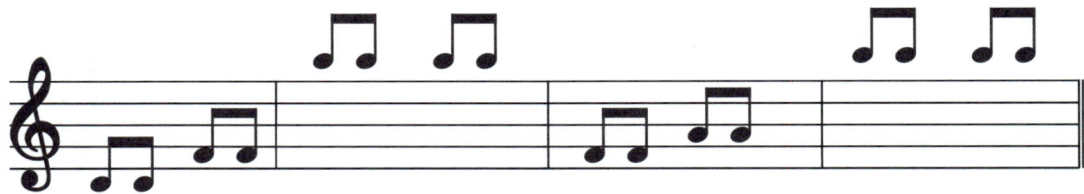

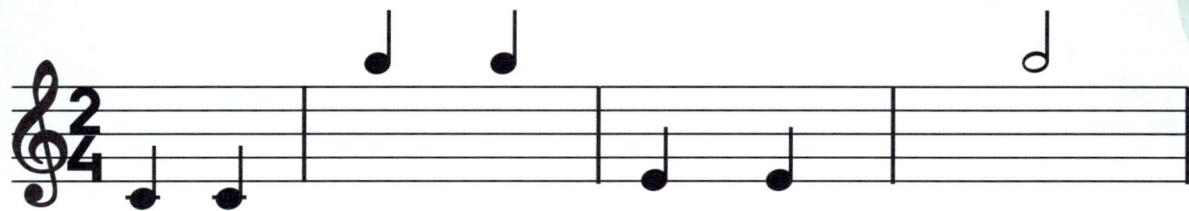
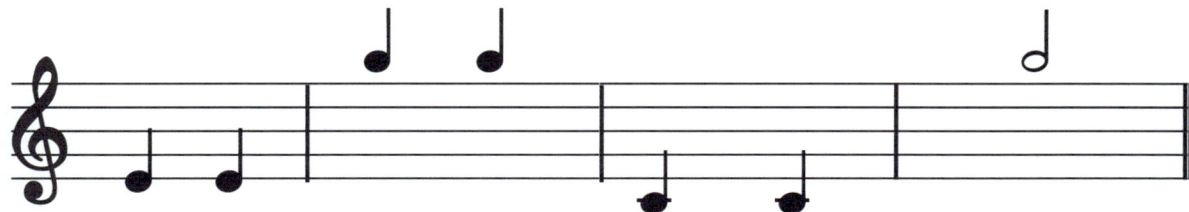

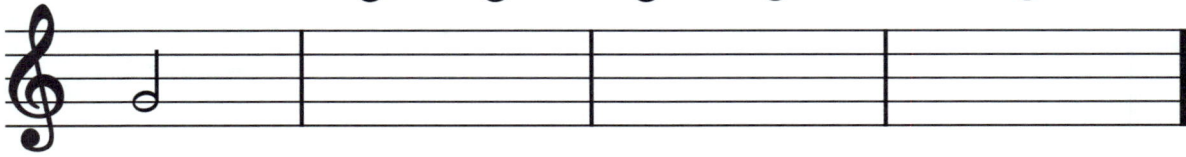

78

Now come up with your own melody

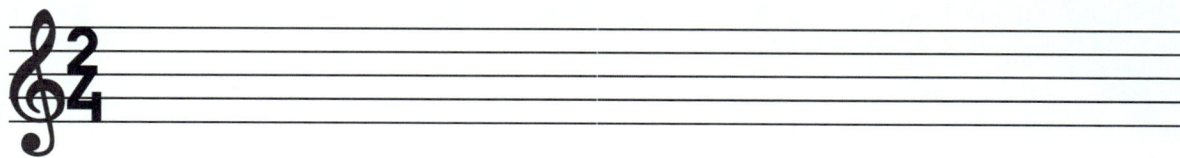

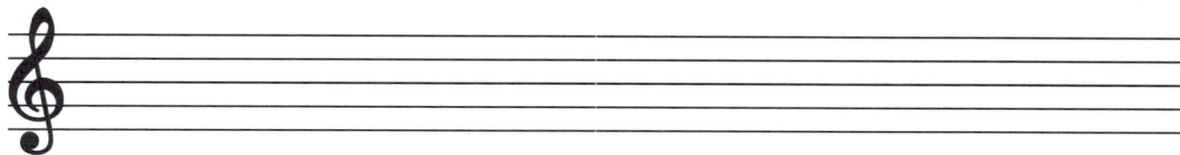

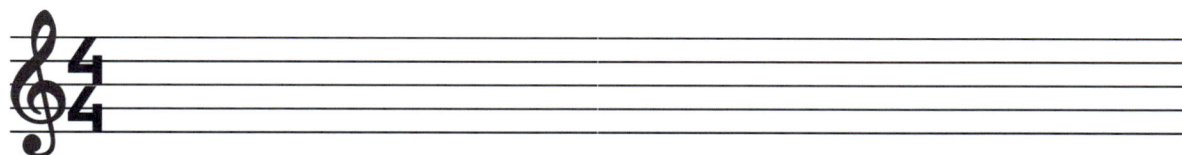

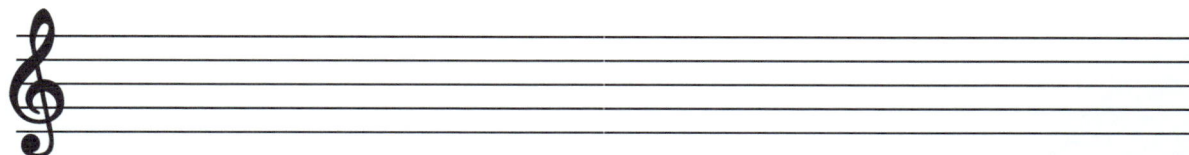

Made in United States
Troutdale, OR
02/06/2025